German Mechanized Infantry on Combat Operations in Afghanistan

Marcel Bohnert & Andy Neumann

German Mechanized Infantry on Combat Operations in Afghanistan

Marcel Bohnert & Andy Neumann

2017
Carola Hartmann Miles-Verlag

Bibliografische Information der Deutschen Nationalbibliothek
Die Deutsche Nationalbibliothek verzeichnet diese Publikation in
der Deutschen Nationalbibliografie; detaillierte bibliografische
Daten sind im Internet über www.dnb.de abrufbar.

© 2017 Carola Hartmann Miles-Verlag
  www.miles-verlag.jimdo.com
  email: miles-verlag@t-online.de

Book Series:
German Veterans Publishing,
Maison d'edition d'anciens combattans
All images:
Soldiers of 2nd Infantry Company, Task Force Kunduz III
Illustrations:
Nathalie Falkowski, Hamburg/Germany
Cover:
Soldiers of 2nd Infantry Company, Task Force Kunduz III on
patrol, 22 August 2011, Western Plate/Chahar Darreh District,
Kunduz Province/Afghanistan © Maurizio Gambarini, dpa,
Berlin/Germany

Herstellung: Books on Demand, Norderstedt

Alle Rechte, insbesondere das Recht der Vervielfältigung und
Verbreitung sowie der Übersetzung, vorbehalten. Kein Teil des
Werkes darf in irgendeiner Form (durch Fotokopie, Mikrofilm
oder ein anderes Verfahren) ohne schriftliche Genehmigung des
Verlages reproduziert oder unter Verwendung elektronischer
Systeme gespeichert, verarbeitet, vervielfältigt oder verbreitet
werden.

Printed in Germany

ISBN 978-3-945861-45-5

**Dedicated to the
New German Combat Veterans**

Contents

(1) Prologue: »Operation Tür« 9
(Kunduz, Afghanistan, September 2011)

(2) Introduction: 11
Challenges of New Wars

(3) How Mechanized Infantry Became 20
Involved in Afghanistan

(4) Deployment of a Mechanized 27
Infantry Company: 200 Days in Kunduz

    4.1 Preparation for Operations 28

    4.2 Course of the Deployment 30

    4.3 Résumé of the Tour of Duty 36

(5) Combat Effectiveness of Mechanized Infantry in Afghanistan	44
(6) Outlook	64
(7) Epilogue (Termez Airfield, Uzbekistan, June 2011)	69

Authors	77
References/German Bibliography	83
List of Abbreviations	94
Additional Information	95

(1) Prologue: »Operation Tür« (Kunduz, Afghanistan, September 2011)

September 9 is a day that many of us will remember for a very long time. It has a special significance for many Afghans, too: it is the national day of remembrance in honor of Ahmad Shah Massoud. The ethnic Tajik became a legend in the late 1980s in the fight against the Soviet army and as the leader of the Mujahideen fighters, and later became a figure symbolizing the resistance against the Taliban. On 9 September 2001, Massoud died in an attack carried out by two suicide bombers disguised as journalists. Shortly thereafter he was officially declared a national hero by the Afghan President.

Exactly ten years later, the engines of German infantry combat and other armored vehicles were to be heard in the northern Afghan province of Kunduz. The Bundeswehr had been involved in the war in the Hindu Kush for almost a decade now. Over the years, the ISAF mission had developed from a humanitarian stabilization operation into a combat mission and has led to casualties among Bundeswehr and other Alliance members. In 2010, the then Major General Hans-Werner Fritz had activated German training and protection battalions which were to operate in the frontline as two fully-equipped task forces: Task Force Kunduz and Task Force Mazar-E-Sharif. By that point at the latest, consideration was finally being given to the changed threat situation at tactical level.

As part of Task Force Kunduz III we began »Operation Tür« in the early morning hours of 9 September 2011 in the troubled district of Chahar Darreh. Our intent was to recover two APC Dingo doors left behind in the small town of Isa Khel since the Good Friday fire fights of 2010. They bore witness to that bloody day on which three German soldiers had died and several others had been wounded in heavy fighting. Aside from the Kunduz bombing in September 2009, Good Friday 2010 is considered to be the break or turning point in how the public perceived Germany's mission there.

Reinforced infantry platoon Bravo, comprising mounted and dismounted forces, was now at the location of those past events. Despite the early hour, the thermometer was already showing more than 40 degrees (100 degrees Fahrenheit), and the heavily laden soldiers were making their way into the small town. Engineers and EOD specialists scanned the ground for booby traps while, under their protection, the armored vehicles pushed on gradually to the river where the company's infantry forces had discovered the doors several weeks before. The dismounted forces conversed with locals and secured the advance of the combat vehicles in all directions. Towards 10:30 hrs, shortly after the arduous recovery of the doors weighing several hundred pounds, the company received information that a combat patrol sent out by the recce company had come under IED attack on the Western Plate of the high plateau near the small town of Nawabad and that German soldiers had been wounded. The operation in Isa Khel was broken off immediately and, after a halt at Hill 432 for coordination purposes during which vital support forces were integrated into already present mechanized infantry platoon Charlie, the alerted forces deployed at full speed to the location of the attack almost ten kilometers (six miles) away. The lead Marder armored infantry combat vehicle (AICV) overheated and broke down at a choke point shortly before reaching the approach to the Western Plate. The Marder following behind pushed it off the road despite the risk of damaging its cooling system, enabling the road march to rapidly continue. During our approach we were escorted by US Black Hawk helicopters that were already in the process of landing and taking on one of the wounded just less than a kilometer (half a mile) away before we reached the site of the attack. Accepting high personal risk, they set down, as they so often do, in a "hot zone", thus ensuring fast medical treatment.

After the AICVs had established a defensive perimeter at the site of the attack, our EOD specialists carried out a search to minimize the threat of secondary IEDs. The accompanying recovery forces from Camp Kunduz loaded the destroyed scout vehicle onto a heavy equipment transporter and then withdrew under our watchful eyes. Contrary to the original operation planning for the company, Bravo platoon then made dispositions to spend the night on the Western Plate and, in poor visibility, conducted light reconnaissance patrols on the outskirts of Nawabad so as to avoid giving the enemy any feeling of triumph. That same night a BM-1 missile fired from the north eastern part of Isa Khel impacted in the immediate vicinity of Camp Kunduz. A post-blast analysis carried out on site on

11 September 2011 together with Afghan security forces yielded no information on the offenders, however. Also that same evening, another missile was fired in the direction of the camp. Consequently, 2nd and 3rd Companies alternately deployed sniper teams accompanied by infantry who took up positions to observe Isa Khel. Although they did not gather any particular reconnaissance information, they did, temporarily at least, prevent further missiles from being fired at the camp.

Soldiers from 2nd Company recovering APC Dingo doors from the small town of Isa Khel where the 2011 Good Friday fighting had taken place.

armored combat vehicles or behind high camp fences. It also meant a particular capability profile and a high level of risk for those troops.

The present book will focus on the deployment of mechanized infantry of the German Armed Forces (or 'Bundeswehr') including Marder AICVs in Afghanistan. It will firstly be discussed how their involvement in the mission came about and then be described what challenges they faced, using the operations of Task Force Kunduz III as an example. Subsequently their combat effectiveness will be considered and possible lessons for them for future missions formulated. The following accounts depict mission experiences as company commander and platoon leader in the northern Afghan province of Kunduz. The book is therefore pragmatic in its approach, and it has to be borne in mind that it tends to reflect the perspective of the military rank and file rather than the political leadership or higher military command.

Engaging with the population and cooperation with the Afghan security forces were the core aspects of the Counterinsurgency (COIN) strategy in Afghanistan.

"Boots on the ground" in Kunduz 2011 – Dismounted patrols also meant greater stress and risk for our soldiers.

(3) How Mechanized Infantry Became Involved in Afghanistan

The Bundeswehr had been taking part in the ISAF mission since 2002 – initially with a force contingent of just 1,200 servicemen and women. What had begun with patrols greeted enthusiastically in Kabul degenerated, in the course of the years in the provinces of Kunduz and Baghlan, into heavy fighting and bloody guerilla warfare. The increasing attacks on German forces first met with incredulity and, later, led to a greater focus on self-protection and to the extent possible, the cessation of operations in dangerous regions. Initial calls for heavier weapons such as mortars, self-propelled howitzers or Tornado jets were rejected from the standpoint that the political strategy was a defensive one. For a long time there were also concerns about deploying AICVs as they were considered a step towards conflict escalation and efforts were being made not to have the German contingent perceived as an occupying force. Other arguments against their field deployment were the bad condition of roads and bridges and the major logistic effort it involved. There were, of course, also understandable doubts due to the system's advanced age: the first of the Marder production vehicles were delivered to Bundeswehr units in 1971 and a desert fighting capability did not, as yet, play any role in its development.

The security situation began to change, and the number of direct attacks on German forces increased steadily, starting 2006. The first four Marder 1A5 AICVs arrived by the turn of 2006/2007 in Mazar-E-Sharif where they were initially used to protect the camp. Their use at that time was still subject to the approval of the Chief of Defense (Generalinspekteur), Bundeswehr, so as to be able to retain strict control over situations in the event of their possible escalation. In view of the steadily deteriorating situation, they were earmarked from mid-2008 onward to support the Quick Reaction Force (QRF) of Regional Command North and, in spring 2009, were deployed to Kunduz where German soldiers were already being confronted with a new quality of insurgent attacks. The Marder AICVs saw their first frontline use in July 2009 when extricating Belgian and Afghan security forces from an ambush. This first combat experience alone demonstrated the enormous effect the AICVs had on enemy forces. Within just a year, the QRF was involved in well over fifty fire-fights and hour-long engagements in which the Marder proved its worth time and again. We will go into the lessons learned with, and merits of its use later on in this book.

The air strike in Kunduz in September 2009 called in by, at that time, Colonel Georg Klein, and the fighting that occurred on Good Friday 2010, made the shift in strategy by the German ground forces in Afghanistan more than clear and also led to a change in political thinking: in quick succession, Heron reconnaissance drones were leased and three type 2000 armored self-propelled howitzers as well as another fifteen Marder AICVs ordered to the Hindu Kush. The combat units of Task Forces Kunduz and Mazar-E-Sharif had, as a result, one mechanized infantry platoon each including major equipment at their disposal from 2010 onwards.

The particular conditions of the dynamic and complex operational environment in Afghanistan called for constant maintenance of the AICV model and led to several upgrades. First of all, 74 Marders were retrofitted between 2002 and 2005 as model 1A5 with protection against blast mines and explosively formed projectiles. This involved clearing the crew compartment floor, modifying the stowage concept, and fastening the seat frame to the hull roof. As the extremely high temperatures inside the vehicle had a major influence on the endurance of the crews, Rheinmetall Landsysteme GmbH also developed a compartment cooling system based on an order awarded in October 2009. The testing conducted by the Bundeswehr Technical Center certified the system as having a positive effect, but it was also pointed out that any fundamental changes to the cooling capacity were hardly possible, as it was a matter of integrating it into equipment that had already been introduced into service. The occurring faults and shortcomings were considered acceptable, though, given the urgent operational need and lack of alternatives. Also among the retrofitted kit was the CG12 jammer which could be used to counter radio-remote-controlled IEDs in close proximity to the AICV. In addition, Saab-Barracuda developed a customized camouflage system designed primarily to provide camouflage and, secondarily, to act as a heat-reducing shield. This, too, was tested by the Bundeswehr Technical Center in 2009 and examined in several driving trials regarding its effectiveness as well as technical and ergonomic system compatibility. After several enhancements, the AICVs already in Afghanistan were retrofitted with the multispectral camouflage system (Barracuda camouflage netting). The first ten Marder 1A5A1 vehicles were delivered in late 2010 and a further 25 retrofitted by the end of 2011.

A renaissance that packs a punch: Marder AICVs in October 2010 in position at the police station in the troubled district of Chahar Darreh.

Kunduz 2011: A Marder AICV taking up an overwatching position in the early morning hours. Upgrades such as the crew compartment cooling system, improvised add-on structures and parts of the Barracuda camouflage netting are visible.

(4) Deployment of a Mechanized Infantry Company: 200 Days in Kunduz

In 2010, German soldiers in Afghanistan were involved in the heaviest fighting since the establishment of the Bundeswehr. At that time, 92 Mechanized Infantry Training Battalion in Munster was given the task of taking on military responsibility as the lead element for just under seven months the following year in the northern Afghanistan province of Kunduz thus becoming part of the 26th and 27th German contingents of ISAF. After eight months of preparation for operations, our 2nd Company, 92 Mechanized Infantry Training Battalion, was the first unit of Task Force Kunduz III to be deployed completely to Afghanistan, and only a few days after its arrival started to patrol the troubled district of Chahar Darreh. What follows gives an insight into the company's conduct and concept of operations during its more than 200 days of deployment.

4.1 Preparation for Operations

Two in-theatre fact-finding missions enabled us to gain an impression of the line companies' situation in Chahar Darreh and, from that, to draw conclusions regarding our own preparation for operations. In early October 2010, paratroop units reinforced by mechanized infantry were engaged in fighting mainly in the southern part of the district. Particularly by taking part in a patrol and spending the night at the local police station, we were able to gather valuable information during that period, not only in regard to the topography, enemy situation or extraordinarily high stress factors for man and material, but also regarding the goals and progress when conducting operations. The first-hand combat reports especially provided an unadorned picture of the new German operational reality, ranging from day-long battles, to bloody skirmishes at grenade-throwing distance, to contact explosions involving IEDs. A glance at the situation map and soldiers' accounts showed that the first Task Force Kunduz could already boast tactical successes at that time. Its units were operating offensively and putting "boots on the ground". Unlike several years previously, our allies could no longer accuse the Bundeswehr of holing up in its camps. The price the Force had to pay, though, was many wounded and traumatized soldiers. The impressions gained were put to use in the pre-deployment training.

Several weeks before the beginning of our deployment, a delegation from the Mechanized Infantry Training Battalion was in Kunduz once more to carry out a last check on the current situation and have our direct predecessors give us an account of recent situation developments. This second fact-finding mission was overshadowed by two bomb attacks in which German members of the Task Force lost their lives or were injured. Nevertheless, upon our arrival the combat units were not in a state of shock, but appeared to be operating at the same high speed. Our predecessors had been able to continue with "Operation Halmazag" in November 2010 and had meanwhile brought large parts of southern Chahar Darreh under their control. Moreover, operations were already being conducted in the north where, admittedly, there were frequent attacks and bombings. So our aim was clear: further stabilization of the southern part of the district and expansion of the "security bubble" toward the north.

4.2   Course of the Deployment

Several attacks during the first six months of 2011 had already cost the lives of seven German soldiers and wounded many others, some of them severely. We saw this as heralding a late summer offensive on the part of the insurgents, and it had an influence on what to expect from our tour of duty. The attacks against the Bundeswehr's forces, however, increasingly tended to take the form of booby traps and to avoid open combat. A further perfidious form of threat also manifested itself in February of the same year, claiming the lives of three German soldiers and causing physical injuries to six others: attacks by insiders, in other words Afghan Security Forces, who turned on their allies. They fueled mistrust and had the potential to undermine troop morale as well as the faith in the sense of the mission. We made do with several measures that were at least able to limit that risk. These included, particularly, building a close relationship of trust with our Afghan allies.

Initial patrols with Afghan police officers started less than a week after the last members of our company had arrived in theatre. First of all, we conducted shorter operations in close proximity to our outpost in Chahar Darreh to enable our soldiers as well as the company command team to acclimatize to the new conditions and develop situational awareness. Extreme outdoor temperatures of more than 50 degrees (Celsius) in the shade demanded extreme physical resilience from each individual. Given the threat situation, there could be no relaxation regarding the wearing of helmets, armor vests or ordnance backpacks. Temperatures inside the Marder AICV rose to 80 degrees (Celsius!), which was almost unbearable, especially for the driver and the gunner in the front crew compartment, and soon reached the limits of what was acceptable. The retrofits provided by industry and the modifications made by the Marder crews were able to improve this situation only to a limited degree. Nonetheless, after just a few days the company was also operating in the midday heat in the southern part of the district and started to patrol the northern part. Over 24 hours, each platoon conducted two patrols lasting several hours during the day- or nighttime, making it possible to quickly achieve a substantial presence in their area of responsibility. At times the company grew to be 250-strong in the field thanks to a large number of combat support forces, and platoon leaders commanded as many as 25 combat vehicles. Such extensive support made it possible to have the reinforced platoons patrol at different locations on a constantly alternating basis and thus ensure an almost continuous presence in Chahar Darreh. Furthermore the company was always able to be present with visible combat power and, by doing so, make a corresponding impression on the population and enemy.

In only our second phase of territorial responsibility, the main focus of our operations shifted to the northern part of the district. Meanwhile we were conducting routine patrols in southern villages and small towns like Isa Khel, Quatliam or Haji Amanulla where, several months before, there would automatically have been engagements with insurgents. Also during our first few patrols in northern Chahar Darreh, the expected attacks failed to materialize, prompting us to increase the frequency of our patrols further and to continuously expand the security bubble northward. Very soon we had established good connections with the population in Nahr-i-Sufi, Sujani or Qara Yatim and were able to piece together more of the operational picture puzzle. We had also cautiously started to patrol the outskirts of a small town that, day by day, attracted our attention: Nawabad. That town with its estimated population of 10,000 to 15,000 inhabitants was regarded as the insurgents' stronghold in the summer months of 2011. Several IED finds and information from Military Intelligence told us that we were not particularly welcome there. Nawabad, however, was the largest town in the whole of Chahar Darreh and there was no way we could ignore it. On the contrary, especially here was the potential to bring about a genuine change in the district. After several day and night patrols by individual subunits of the company and countless reconnaissance flights by drones, the time had come for the company to carry out its first operations spanning several days. We had planned special tactics for this: we would not, as previously, patrol from the outside into Nawabad, but set up our command posts in the middle of the town and operate from there. We together with the Afghan security forces established defensive positions at several homesteads within Nawabad and from those "safe houses" carried out patrols in every area of the town. Only one platoon remained permanently stationed on the adjacent Western Plate of the desert plateau, to serve as a reserve if required. This approach, which we repeated several times and intensified in the course of our deployment, offered several advantages: firstly, our constant presence in Nawabad enabled us to cultivate a continuous exchange with the population. There were hardly any time constraints like there had otherwise been regarding the duration of patrols due to the limited availability of helicopters, drones or jet fighters. Our uninterrupted presence made it possible to heighten the feeling of security among the population, as the danger of reprisals by insurgents diminished. Moreover, we were able to patrol any area of Nawabad at any time, without any discernible preparation. This unpredictability made it difficult for enemy forces to adapt to us and take possible countermeasures. It did not fail to leave an impression on the enemy, who at no time ventured to engage us in open battle, yet repeatedly made life difficult for us by emplacing IEDs. We succeeded in finding many of these IEDs. In no case did they kill or even injure members of the company. After several weeks, the pressure exerted on the insurgents by conducting this sort of operation also brought about something referred to by an American journalist as the "squeeze effect", confirmed later by Military Intelligence – a massive exodus of enemy forces to a neighboring district. This was one of our greatest successes during our tour of duty. The way toward the north of Chahar Darreh had been prepared. By the end of our tour of duty we had patrolled in nearly all of the more than seventy villages and small towns in the district several times and established links to the population. Only once were elements of the company drawn into a fire fight. On another occasion, an explosive device detonated in the midst of a patrolling platoon. This stands in contrast to seventeen IED finds and the disposal of countless unexploded munitions and ammunition scrap. On top of this there was the positive assessment by our sister company, which operated on a regular basis in Chahar Darreh during our regeneration period and with whom we carried out Task Force operations, like "Desert Dragon" in November 2011, under the command of the battalion commander. By the end of the contingent's tour of duty in early 2012, freedom of movement had largely been established throughout the district.

4.3　Résumé of the Tour of Duty

Considered as tactical achievements of Task Force Kunduz III are, among others, the considerable progress made by Afghan Security Forces in exercising responsibility for security, the establishment of extensive freedom of movement in northern Chahar Darreh, the taking of the small town of Nawabad, and the prevention of the insurgents from staging a summer offensive in our area of responsibility. Not forgetting our predecessors' achievements, the professionalism of our servicemen and women and the necessary modicum of soldier's luck were also crucial in this respect. We took an offensive yet considered approach, patrolled frequently and at very different times outside the outposts, and probed in-depth. On several occasions we conducted company and Task Force operations during which soldiers were in the field for up to nine days without interruption. By doing so we deprived the enemy of the chance to take the initiative. Only once were forces of 2nd Company embroiled in a firefight. The insurgents were otherwise forced to resort to their perfidious tactic of emplacing booby traps. They succeeded only three times in carrying out IED strikes against forces of Task Force Kunduz:

once against infantry platoon Alpha, once against mechanized infantry platoon Golf, and once against a combat patrol of the reconnaissance company. That is relatively little compared to the high number of booby traps detected by our own units.

During the handover phases in January 2012 we communicated the "spirit" in which our operations had been conducted to our successors and advised on possible ways to proceed. They, too, were able to gain an impression of our progress during their preliminary fact-finding trips and attune their pre-deployment preparations accordingly. As already 200 days previously, the Task Force commander saw it as important during the hand-over to have a seamless transition in the conduct of operations and to provide the new forces swiftly with information, equipment and materiel. In mid-January 2012 a line company of Task Force Kunduz IV assumed territorial responsibility in Chahar Darreh for the first time. It was to be the last of its kind. The just under two-year history of the training and protection battalions was brought to an end with the transition to the Partnering and Advisory Task Force structure from mid-2012 onward.

The crest of our unit: blue is the color of 2nd Company, "L" stands for the affiliation with 9 Armor Training Brigade and 92 Mechanized Infantry Training Battalion and the falcon, being a proud creature, symbolizes our respect for the Afghan population and the Afghan security forces.

Dismounted Belgian troops escorted by AICVs of Charlie platoon at the start of an offensive by 2nd Company in Nawabad.

Controlled detonation of an IED during a company operation in the northern part of the Chahar Darreh district, observed from an outpost.

Mechanized infantry could also be employed in a purely infantry role without any problems: here on foot patrol in scorching heat, north of Nawabad.

A flock of sheep passes an overwatching position taken up by Charlie platoon of the mechanized infantry in southern Chahar Darreh.

Farewell extended by the commander of Task Force Kunduz III to Captain Marcel Bohnert. In front of the grove of honor of 2nd Company at Kunduz camp, the recovered Dingo doors found their place as a reminder of those killed and wounded among our predecessor contingents.

(5) Combat Effectiveness of Mechanized Infantry in Afghanistan

To determine the combat effectiveness of mechanized infantry equipped with the Marder AICV, we would first like to consider the organizational structure of our company and then the advantages and disadvantages that emerged during the Afghanistan mission from our viewpoint. We will also take a look at the lessons learned by other contingents and, for example, at the value of modifications made to the AICVs, as well as at tactical aspects.

The two combat units that made up Task Force Kunduz III were generated from the 2nd and 3rd Company of 92 Mechanized Infantry Training Battalion. Our task as company commanders was to set up the mechanized infantry companies some eight months before the start of the mission so that we would not exceed the personnel ceiling of 128 soldiers in either case and also take into account the training level of our forces, the tactical approach taken by our predecessors, and the major equipment available in theatre. We agreed on a uniform structure: two infantry platoons (with a strength of 35 soldiers each), a mechanized infantry platoon (strength: 12 soldiers) and a sniper section (strength: 12 soldiers) were generated in both companies, to be available as a fourth maneuver unit. This structure proved very successful with regard to our mission in Kunduz. The criticism often voiced beforehand that the mechanized infantry platoons would be reduced to "remaining under armor" because of their low dismounted strength was not confirmed in any way during our mission. The advantage of the AICV crews having greater sustainability through the possibility of taking along sufficient equipment, ammunition and supplies outweighed this, in our opinion, and even increased the combat effectiveness of the mechanized infantry platoon, especially where operations lasting several days were concerned. Nonetheless, reducing the infantry platoons by one squad each and reinforcing the AICV crews with two infantry vehicles to increase the dismounted strength was a possible course of action that was occasionally used. It was also possible to reinforce infantry platoons with AICVs so as to give them long-range weapons and adequate fire power. "Pulling them apart" remained the exception, however, so as to exploit the full effectiveness of the subunits. Depending on the situation, using the mechanized infantry platoon together with snipers or engineers was also an option.

One of the major advantages of using AICVs in Afghanistan was their psychological impact – on the population, on our Afghan partners and on enemy forces. They could be seen as a convincing demonstration of our will to fight the insurgents and protect the local population. As part of their 'show of force' they could even intimidate the enemy at great distances through track and engine noises. Also, as combat reports of previous contingents had shown, the insurgents initially underestimated the range and fire power of the on-board weapons, the armor protection and the observation resources of the AICVs completely.

We often used the mechanized infantry platoon to watch over other subunits from elevated positions, which quite certainly was an impressive sight for enemy forces. Its effect on the fighting morale of the monitored or otherwise supported units cannot be rated highly enough, either. The combination of fire power, armor protection and mobility was a quality which also proved its worth at the Hindu Kush very quickly. The AICVs always ensured rapid headway in difficult terrain. Downsizing of the AICV crews to six soldiers created a lot of stowage space, enabling us to deploy the mechanized infantry platoon completely self-sufficiently and without resupply for up to eight days in the field.

While Afghan clay walls simply absorbed the 5.56 mm and 7.62 mm small arms ammunition, the shells from the 20 mm vehicle rapid-fire weapon system and the "Milan" guided antitank weapon were able to penetrate them without any major problems. The AICV itself was also able to break through walls and create entry points for use by infantry and other combat vehicles. The fire team, when in position above the hatch, was able to observe and bring effect to bear through 360 degrees, which was a crucial advantage especially in the unclear threat environment in Afghanistan. By making improvised modifications we had upgraded the Marder AICVs with sandbags, jute and Hesco gabions into mobile emplacements that offered sufficient protection for the crew and effective possibilities to use their small arms and munitions. During movements by road, other traffic kept a clear distance to our AICVs – unlike when we used wheeled vehicles – which provided additional protection against accidents and suicide attackers. And last but not least, the Marder's gap-crossing and deep-fording capability as well as its capacity to cross waterways also stood it in good stead. Mechanized infantry were thus able to cross the Kunduz River even at locations where the company's infantry, mounted on Dingo and Fuchs armored transport vehicles, had greater problems.

One initial disadvantage was that some tracks and roads in Kunduz Province were unsuitable for the AICVs to drive on. Narrow alleys between clay walls and unstable bridges made careful planning of operations and accurate interpretation of aerial images taken from drones and other aircraft indispensable. The weather and terrain conditions in Afghanistan also put considerable strain on personnel and materiel. By deciding to crew each vehicle with only six soldiers, we made the situation somewhat more bearable, although the temperatures of up to 80 degrees Celsius inside the vehicles called for enormous resilience, especially from the drivers and gunners. Without easing the regulations on the wearing of uniforms inside the crew compartments, which also meant greater personal risk for those soldiers, nobody would have been able to accomplish that mission. Although the retrofitted cooling system was useful, it repeatedly failed on some vehicles and was therefore hardly any help to some armored vehicle crews. It also limited the fording capability of the Marder which, in turn, had to be taken into consideration when planning operations. The high outdoor temperatures additionally caused AICVs to break down, especially in the summer months, because the engine cooling systems were not designed for the desert-like conditions, and difficulties with burst cooling hoses, for example, arose as a result.

The official upgrades, self-made emplacements and the other modifications were indispensable to accomplish the mission, although they also increased the combat weight of the AICVs considerably. This firstly meant that, in phases where the density of operational assignments was high, it was necessary to replace the track pads completely after just a few days. The wear and tear on the tracks and suspension system was extremely high. Secondly, the add-on structures and numerous items of equipment considerably restricted the protection provided against mines. It was impossible to use the stowage space in a way that weapons, ammunition and equipment would not become dangerous projectiles in the event of an IED strike. We had to accept that risk, however. At the start of our mission we had received brand-new, modified Marder 1A5A1 AICVs from the depot in Kunduz and had spontaneously decided how to prepare the combat vehicles. Many things needed consideration in this respect, ranging from engaging the enemy via the top-rear hatches, stowing the complete combat load, accessing ordnance and ammunition, or transporting field beds, to options for rapid preparation of recovery measures, sun and weather protection, the stowage of gas bottles, pans, personal equipment and add-on units such as the "Mikado" tactical helicopter drone, to the supply of water and food, or possibilities to answer the call of nature. Every space, no matter how small, had to be used and particularly the interior of the vehicles planned precisely in order to be sustainable and also be able to assure the best possible protection against mines.

It must additionally be noted that the optical systems of the AICV were only of limited use. The thermal imaging and Peri-Z11 observation systems were antiquated and ageing, allowing only a small degree of magnification and sometimes forcing the gunners to assume an uncomfortable and strenuous body posture for hours, especially during nighttime monitoring and site security missions.

When weighing up the arguments for and against the use of AICVs in Afghanistan, and if the lessons learned by other task forces are considered, the conclusion is reached – like we did – that the Marder's presence was extremely beneficial and, overall, proved very effective. With its weaponry and its martial appearance, it gave the fighting force in Kunduz exactly what it urgently needed from 2009 onward. Not only the lessons learned from our contingent's tour of duty demonstrated that the Marder was versatile, led to a high level of sustainability and significantly enhanced the combat capability of the field units. Well-trained vehicle crews with many years of experience were totally familiar with the vehicle and knew how to repair it themselves in the event of minor technical breakdowns, thus maintaining the operational readiness of their units and subunits. A system incorporating more complicated technology and electrical components might have led to higher failure rates and other limitations. The advantages, in our opinion, very clearly outweighed the negative aspects that have been mentioned.

One advantage of deploying mechanized infantry in Afghanistan so far mentioned only between the lines was that they were not only skilled in mounted combat with their AICVs but could also be employed in a purely infantry role. Coordinating mounted and dismounted forces is one of the core skills of mechanized infantry, and so integrating numerous combat support forces was not a real problem for us, either at company or platoon level. Understanding mounted and dismounted interaction with other forces – be they engineers, artillerymen, drone crews, medical personnel, Female Engagement Teams or the Route Clearance Package – was of vital importance during the Afghanistan mission. It is even possible to conclude from these experiences that mechanized infantry are the Bundeswehr's branch of service with the highest combat effectiveness in asymmetric and hybrid conflicts.

Break from operations: the members of mechanized infantry platoon Charlie await further orders from their platoon leader at an outpost.

The soldiers of mechanized infantry platoon Charlie have set up emplacements on the rear crew compartments of their Marder AICVs, turning them into "mobile fortresses".

Extreme climatic conditions were experienced in all their facets during our tour of duty: Marder AICV in the snow at the onset of winter in Kunduz in November 2011.

Master Sergeant Andy Neumann as platoon leader of mechanized infantry platoon Charlie in 2nd Company of Task Force Kunduz III.

Fighting the dust and heat: view from the rear crew compartment of an AICV during a company operation in Kunduz in 2011.

The all-terrain Marder AICV proved to be extremely effective in the difficult terrain of Afghanistan. Seen from a distance, however, its rear seemed to "sag" a little because of its additional combat weight.

Mobile emplacements: some modifications made to the Marder AICV in Afghanistan were improvised and carried out by the field units themselves.

Each fire team member was allowed to set up his/her fighting position on the Marder individually in regard to rifle rests and arrangement of ordnance and ammunition.

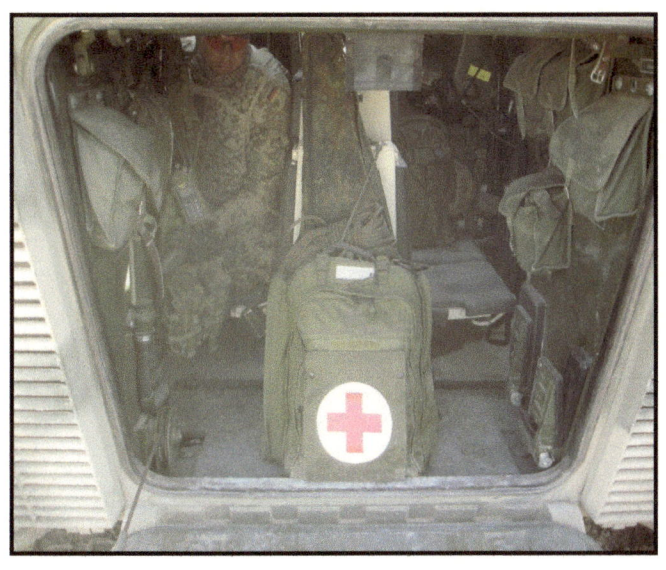

Creativity and improvisation: to provide space for the indispensable medical backpacks, the soldiers removed the squad leader seats on all the AICVs of Charlie platoon.

To create rifle rests, cover and further stowage space on the AICVs, Hesco gabions were cut to shape, fastened to the AICVs, partially filled with sandbags and then lined with jute cloth.

Interacting with infantry forces, mechanized infantry on Marder AICVs displayed their greatest fighting effectiveness in Afghanistan.

(6) Outlook

With, at times, 5,500 German military personnel serving in theatre, the Bundeswehr was the third largest troop contributor in Afghanistan, and has been shaped and changed enormously over the past decade. The successive phases of that mission can be categorized as: providing assistance, taking casualties, and resorting to combat operations. These categories stand in stark contrast to one another, yet illustrate that our armed forces have had to face numerous new challenges and scenarios and underwent a learning process in many areas. Bundeswehr military personnel in Afghanistan showed themselves capable of a whole spectrum of tasks. They were confronted with a multitude of challenges relating to the system of norms and values prevailing in a foreign country, their own hybrid role as aid workers, mediators and fighters, or the difficult return to their home environment. Besides many improvements in terms of equipment, structure and care for wounded and traumatized personnel as well as for surviving relatives, there have meanwhile been a number of positive developments at cultural level. Shared hardships and extreme experiences have seen the emergence of a self-assured and empowered "generation of mission veterans".

Many no longer believed that the Marder armored infantry combat vehicle would experience a renaissance in the Afghanistan hostilities. It was already threatening to fall into disrepute as a relic of the Cold War before it was demonstrated in the ISAF mission that it would remain a reliable, tried and combat-tested weapon system, offering high operational effectiveness, until its successor was fully ready for service. The first Puma infantry combat vehicles have already been fielded, and many vehicle crews are now being trained on them. Of these new systems, 350 are due to be delivered to the Bundeswehr by 2025, thus finally bringing to an end the successful story of the Marder AICV in the mechanized infantry after more than 50 years.

Any large-scale deployment like the Afghanistan mission seems unlikely for the Bundeswehr and its allies in the foreseeable future. It has become clear, however, since the statements made in concert by Germany's Federal President, Foreign Minister and Defense Minister at the Munich Security Conference in 2014, at the very latest, that Germany will continue to help in resolving crises and conflicts around the world and play an active role in foreign and security policy. Because of international terrorism, flows of refugees and the threat to trade routes, New Wars will have global repercussions and also determine the course of German security and defense policy. The ongoing crisis between the Russian Federation and the Ukraine has meanwhile led to a greater focus on hybrid warfare, which combines the asymmetric scenarios of new wars with the conventional threat posed by regular armed forces, thus blurring the boundaries between state and non-state actions.

ISAF's transition to the Resolute Support (RS) Mission in early 2015 officially brought the chapter of the Bundeswehr's combat mission in Afghanistan to an end. Yet, even during train, assist and advice missions, direct attacks on Bundeswehr members are still possible, while suicide bombers and insiders pose an ever-present latent threat. It is very difficult in practice to distinguish between missions taking place to provide purely logistic, medical and humanitarian support and combat missions. In view of there being vague, spatially and temporally unbounded risks that lend themselves inadequately to operationalization, gradual 'mission creep' is possible – as in Afghanistan – which can also, invariably, lead to heavy fighting, accompanied by fatalities and wounding.

More than 50 Bundeswehr members lost their lives at the Hindu Kush, 35 of those as a result of attacks and combat. Over 300 were wounded and many more were traumatized. Even though Task Force Kunduz III had no loss of life, the Afghanistan mission was also extraordinarily demanding for us and our servicemen and women when it came to fulfilling any official and soldierly duties. The job profile for military commanders on deployment does not differ fundamentally, in our opinion, from that of daily routine duty in the homeland. The decisive difference is that, upon arrival in theatre, the time for exercising and practicing is over, and even the slightest error can have serious consequences. As well as physical robustness, a high level of mental fitness is therefore necessary. Not only to interpret and implement orders correctly, but also to be completely focused and mission-ready when leaving the camp. That permanent alertness and constant thinking about the mission, the surroundings, and protecting one's own soldiers really takes it out of you.

That becomes noticeable, at the latest, after arriving back on home soil.

We would like to conclude our contribution with an epilogue aimed at reminding of the risks to which our servicemen and women are exposed on missions abroad. May the memory of incidents such as these help us never to forget the lessons learned from ISAF. We owe that not least to our fallen comrades, surviving relatives and veterans.

(7) Epilogue
(Termez Airfield, Uzbekistan, June 2011)

Exhausted, we sit at the airfield of the Uzbek border town of Termez. All German contingent members make for the Bundeswehr base here before being flown into Afghanistan, and when leaving the country on the way home. Just finished is another fact-finding visit we have made a few weeks before the start of our tour of duty as Task Force Kunduz III to our direct predecessors. It has been overshadowed by the death of Captain Markus Matthes who, several days before our arrival, was killed by an IED strike in Chahar Darreh. The damaged combat vehicles have been recovered and could be seen for a few more days at the perimeter fence of the camp. This was the new tactic of the insurgents in northern Afghanistan: Only a year ago they had engaged in open combat with ISAF; but now they were resorting more and more to attacks with booby traps – a change in the threat situation which also had to be made clear to our soldiers once again in the last days of their training. Immersed in thought, we compare notes and imagine what it will probably be like here with our company in less than a month. In the meantime, a senior staff officer enters the waiting area and tells all those present to line up at the edge of the airfield. We look at each other somewhat taken aback, but then pack our kit quickly and follow his instruction like all the others. Some minutes later he appears again and tells us he will now lead us onto the maneuvering area. We are still surprised, but march as ordered a few hundred meters to an open area. Upon seeing two aircraft there standing opposite one another, it suddenly dawns on us why we are about to line up in a formation comprising over 100 soldiers that is moving towards those aircraft. Most of the others apparently realize this, too, because it suddenly becomes depressingly quiet. The realization hits us that, in a few moments, we will be providing the honor cordon for the repatriation of a fallen comrade. At the beginning of June a powerful IED containing more than 200 kilograms of explosive had torn apart a Marder AICV in Baghlan province, killing the 23 year-old driver, Corporal Alexej Kobelew, and wounding five other crew members, some of them seriously. We now stand in Termez and pay the fallen comrade our last respects. We raise our hand in military salute as his coffin is transferred from a Transall to an Airbus aircraft. He will be flying back with us to Germany. We will exit Cologne-Wahn Airport on the one side. There, excitedly waving relatives will gleefully embrace their homecomers. His coffin will exit the airport at a different location. Away from the public eye and media circus, surviving relatives will be there to meet him.

The Destroyed Marder AICV: Pul-E-Khumri, Baghlan/Afghanistan, 2 June 2011 (Screenshot US MEDEVAC Video/Helmet Camera).

In memory of fallen soldiers

Authors

Bohnert, Marcel, Major; diploma in educational theory; born in 1979; attended the National General/Admiral Staff Officer Course of the Bundeswehr (LGAN 2015) at the Bundeswehr Command and Staff College in Hamburg; formerly section leader in Task Force Zur, Kosovo; officer commanding a combat unit with Task Force Kunduz in Afghanistan, and head of a military section at Bundeswehr University, Hamburg; author of numerous articles concerning the ISAF mission as well as editor of the much-discussed anthologies "Armee im Aufbruch" (Armed Forces on the Move), "Die unsichtbaren Veteranen" (The Unseen Veterans), and the mission report "200 Tage Kunduz" (200 Days Kunduz).

Major (DEU) Marcel Bohnert

Chahar Darreh, Kunduz/Afghanistan, 2011

Neumann, Andy, Master Sergeant; born in 1975; platoon leader during the fielding of the Puma infantry combat vehicle; formerly platoon leader of mechanized infantry platoon Charlie in 2nd Company with Task Force Kunduz III operating in Afghanistan from June 2011 to January 2012; NCO representative on the executive committee of the German Circle of Friends of the Mechanized Infantry Force.

Master Sergeant (DEU) Andy Neumann
Chahar Darreh, Kunduz/Afghanistan, 2011

References/German Bibliography Concerning the Deployment of Mechanized Infantry in Kunduz/Afghanistan:

Blasberg, Anita & Willeke, Stefan (2010): Afghanistan. Das Kundus-Syndrom. Die Zeit, 4 March 2010.

Blumröder, Christian v. (2015): Shape, Clear, Hold, Build – Die Operation Halmazag des Ausbildungs- und Schutzbataillons Kunduz, in: R. Schroeder/ S. Hansen (ed.): Stabilisierungseinsätze als gesamtstaatliche Aufgabe Erfahrungen und Lehren aus dem deutschen Afghanistaneinsatz zwischen Staatsaufbau und Aufstandsbewältigung (COIN). Nomos: Baden-Baden.

Brinkmann, Sascha, Hoppe, Joachim & Schröder, Wolfgang (ed.)(2013): Feindkontakt. Gefechtsberichte aus Afghanistan. Mittler: Hamburg.

Brinkmann, Sascha & Hoppe Joachim (2010): Generation Einsatz. Fallschirmjäger berichten ihre Erfahrungen aus Afghanistan. Miles: Berlin.

Bohnert, Marcel (2017): Die deutsche Bundeswehr und der Einsatz in Afghanistan. Ein kritischer Blick auf die Bewährung der Inneren Führung. Österreichische Militärzeitschrift (in preparation).

Bohnert, Marcel & Schreiber, Björn (ed.)(2016): Die unsichtbaren Veteranen. Kriegsheimkehrer in der deutschen Gesellschaft. Miles: Berlin.

Bohnert, Marcel (2015): COIN an der Basis. Zur Umsetzung des Konzeptes in einer Kampfkompanie der Task Force Kunduz, in: R. Schroeder/S. Hansen (ed.): Stabilisierungseinsätze als gesamtstaatliche Aufgabe Erfahrungen und Lehren aus dem deutschen Afghanistaneinsatz zwischen Staatsaufbau und Aufstandsbewältigung (COIN). Nomos : Baden-Baden, pp. 245-258.

Bohnert, Marcel & Schreiber, Björn (2014): 200 Tage Kunduz Erfahrungen einer Kampfkompanie in Afghanistan. (Photo) presentation, discussion. 3rd edition. Double DVD and video. Helmut Schmidt University/Bundeswehr University Hamburg: Hamburg.

Bohnert, Marcel (2014a): Feinde in den eigenen Reihen. Zur Problematik von Innentätern in Afghanistan. If. Zeitschrift für Innere Führung, 2, pp. 5-12.

Bohnert, Marcel (2014b): Wächter aus der Luft. Drohnen als Schutzpatrone deutscher Bodentruppen in Afghanistan, in: U. Hartmann/C.v. Rosen (ed.): Jahrbuch Innere Führung 2014. Drohnen, Roboter und Cyborgs. Der Soldat im Angesicht neuer Militärtechnologien. Berlin: Miles, pp. 19-34.

Bohnert, Marcel (2014c): Warum ich Soldat bleibe. Loyal – Magazin für Sicherheitspolitik, 10, p. 24-26.

Bohnert, Marcel (2014d): Zur Notwendigkeit lagebezogener Einsatzregeln für Soldatinnen und Soldaten in Auslandsmissionen, in: F. Forster/S. Vugrin/L. Wessendorff (ed.): Das Zeitalter der Einsatzarmee. Herausforderungen für Recht und Ethik. Berlin: Berliner Wissenschafts-Verlag, pp. 131-140.

Bohnert, Marcel (2013a): Armee in zwei Welten, in: M. Böcker/L. Kempf/F. Springer (ed.): Soldatentum. Auf der Suche nach Identität und Berufung der Bundeswehr heute. Olzog: Munich, pp. 75-89.

Bohnert, Marcel (2013b): Die Multiformträger. Anmerkungen zur Anzugordnung in Afghanistan. Der Panzergrenadier, 34, pp. 35-37.

Bohnert, Marcel (2012a): 200 Tage Task Force Kunduz. Einsatzverlauf in der 2. Infanteriekompanie. Der Panzergrenadier, 33, pp. 67-75.

Bohnert, Marcel (2012b): Gemischte Patrouille in Kunduz. Ein schweißtreibender Auftrag. Pioniere – Magazin der Pioniertruppe und des Bundes Deutscher Pioniere, 6, pp. 14-16.

Bohnert, Marcel (2012c): Von Kunduz nach Munster. Einsatzresümee der 2. Kompanie. Der Panzergrenadier, 32, pp. 64-66.

Bohnert, Marcel, Dohmeyer, Floris & Schröder, Friedrich (2011): Aufstellung und Ausbildung einer Infanteriekompanie für die Task Force Kunduz. Der Panzergrenadier, 29, pp. 61-65.

Bohnert, Marcel & Schröder, Friedrich (2011): Ein Einsatz, zwei Welten. Drinnies und Draußies in Afghanistan. Zu gleich – Zeitschrift der Artillerietruppe. 2, pp. 6-9.

Bohnert, Marcel (2011): In der heißen Zone. Die ersten Monate der 2. Infanteriekompanie im Kunduz. Der Panzergrenadier, 30, pp. 37-42.

Brügner, Gunnar, Grohmann, Hans-Christoph & Hecht, Jan (2010): Schützenpanzer Marder 1A5: Erfahrungen aus dem Einsatz. Strategie & Technik, 6, pp. 51-64.

Buske, Rainer (2016): Anforderungen an den militärischen Führer im Einsatz, in: M. Bohnert/B. Schreiber (ed.): Die unsichtbaren Veteranen. Kriegsheimkehrer in der deutschen Gesellschaft, pp. 59-70.

Buske, Rainer (2015): Kunduz. Ein Erlebnisbericht über einen militärischen Einsatz der Bundeswehr in Afghanistan im Jahre 2008. Miles: Berlin.

Chauvistré, Eric & Bangert, Christoph (2012): Auf Montage. NEON, 1, pp. 20-30.

Cihar, Jan (2010): Die 2./PzGrenBtl 122 im Einsatz als 2./Infanteriekompanie PRT Kunduz. Der Panzergrenadier, 28, pp. 77-79.

Clair, Johannes (2014): Geleitwort, in: M. Bohnert/ L.J. Reitstetter (ed.): Armee im Aufbruch. Zur Gedankenwelt junger Offiziere in den Kampftruppen der Bundeswehr. Miles: Berlin, pp. 13-14.

Clair, Johannes (2012): Vier Tage im November. Mein Kampfeinsatz in Afghanistan. Econ: Berlin.

Friederichs, Hauke (2011): Die Kämpfer schimpfen auf die Lagerbürokraten. Die Zeit, 4 February 2011.

Gambarini, Maurizio (2011): Hoffnung für Afghanistan. Bundeswehr aktuell, 19 November 2011, p. 11.

Grohmann, Hans-Christoph (2011): Führung im Gefecht. Erfahrungen und Gedanken zur Verantwortung und Belastung des militärischen Führers. Der Infanterist, 29, pp. 21-27.

Hecht, Jan (2013): Das Wertvollste an der Front. Loyal – Magazin für Sicherheitspolitik, 3, pp. 12-15.

Hilmes, Rolf (2011): 40 Jahre Schützenpanzer Marder. Strategie & Technik, 5, pp. 21-24.

Holz, Nicolas (2010): Die verstärkte 2./Quick Reaction Force 4 in Kunduz. Der Infanterist, 28, pp. 28-32.

Janke, Ralf (2012): Erprobung und Abnahme Raumkühlanlage SPz Marder 1A5. Erprobungsbericht/ Abschlussbericht. BAAINBw/WTD41: Trier

Janke, Ralf (2010): Überprüfung Multispektrale Tarnabdeckung SPz Marder 1A5. Erprobungsbericht/Abschlussbericht. BAAINBw/WTD41: Trier.

Krüger, Thomas (2010): Vom Kampf in Kunduz. Y – Magazin der Bundeswehr, 4, pp. 68-70.

Kuhn, Marc (2014): Über den Horizont. Ansichten eines Laufbahnverräters, in: M. Bohnert/ L.J. Reitstetter (ed.): Armee im Aufbruch. Zur Gedankenwelt junger Offiziere in den Kampftruppen der Bundeswehr. Miles: Berlin, pp. 41-52.

Lindemann, Marc (2015): Rückblick auf einen Krieg. Y – Magazin der Bundeswehr, 2, pp. 26-33.

Mann, Robert Clifford (2014): German Warriors, in: M. Daxner (ed.): Deutschland in Afghanistan. BIS: Oldenburg, pp. 139-153.

Matz, Michael (2011): Jägerregiment 1. Im Einsatz als Quick Reaction Force RC North. Strategie & Technik, 1, pp. 20-24.

Münch, Philipp (2015): Die Bundeswehr in Afghanistan. Militärische Handlungslogik in internationalen Interventionen. Rombach: Freiburg i.Br.

Noetzel, Timo & Rid, Thomas (2009): Germany´s Options in Afghanistan. Survival, 5, pp. 71-90.

Nowitzki, Manja (2012): Die Angst ist täglicher Begleiter. Schweriner Volkszeitung/Nordkurier, 24 January 2012, p. 3.

Piener, Michael (2009): Der I. Zug der 4./PzGrenBtl 122 im Einsatz als H-Zug der I. Infanteriekompanie PRT Kunduz. Der Panzergrenadier, 28, pp. 80-83.

Reichelt, Julian & Meyer, Jan (2010): Ruhet in Frieden, Soldaten! Wie Politik und Bundeswehr die Wahrheit über Afghanistan vertuschen. Fackelträger: Cologne.

Reuter, Christoph & Mettelsiefen, Marcel (2010): Foxtrott auf Höhe 432. Stern, 8, pp. 42-49.

Rippl, Jan (2015): Noch lange kein Alteisen. Y – Das Magazin der Bundeswehr, 1, pp. 30-35.

Rogge Ronald & Rippl, Jan (2011): Trügerische Idylle. Y – Das Magazin der Bundeswehr, 11, pp. 28-35.

Sangar, Eric (2015): The Weight of the Past(s): The Impact of Bundeswehr´s Use of Historical Experience on Strategy-Making in Afghanistan. Journal of Strategic Studies, 4, pp. 411-444.

Schmidt, Michael (2010): Leben am Limit. Der Tagesspiegel, 19 December 2010.

Schnitt, Jonathan (2012): Foxtrott 4. Sechs Monate mit deutschen Soldaten in Afghanistan. Bertelsmann: Munich.

Schreiber, Björn (2015): Zivil-militärische Zusammenarbeit aus der Perspektive eines CIMIC-

Truppführers, in: R. Schroeder/S. Hansen (ed.): Stabilisierungseinsätze als gesamtstaatliche Aufgabe Erfahrungen und Lehren aus dem deutschen Afghanistaneinsatz zwischen Staatsaufbau und Aufstandsbewältigung (COIN). Nomos: Baden-Baden.

Schreiber, Björn & Bohnert, Marcel (2015): Interkulturelle Kompetenz im Kontext Afghanistans. DVD and video. Helmut Schmidt University/Bundeswehr University Hamburg: Hamburg.

Schroeder, Robin & Hansen, Stefan (ed.)(2015): Stabilisierungseinsätze als gesamtstaatliche Aufgabe Erfahrungen und Lehren aus dem deutschen Afghanistaneinsatz zwischen Staatsaufbau und Aufstandsbewältigung (COIN). Nomos: Baden-Baden.

Schwitalla, Artur (2010): Afghanistan, jetzt weiß ich erst... Gedanken aus meiner Zeit als Kommandeur des Provincial Reconstruction Team Feyzabad. Miles: Berlin.

Seiffert, Anja & Heß, Julius (2012): Afghanistan: Ein Einsatz verändert die Bundeswehr. Erkenntnisse aus dem Einsatz des 22. deutschen ISAF-Kontingents. If. Zeitschrift für Innere Führung, 2, p. 20-24.

Seliger, Marco & Ratermann, Jonas (2016): Ein zermürbender Krieg. Loyal – Magazin für Sicherheitspolitik, 10, pp. 8-20.

Seliger, Marco (2013): Lektionen des Krieges. Loyal – Magazin für Sicherheitspolitik, 5, pp. 14-21.

Seliger, Marco (2011a): Bundeswehr in Afghanistan. Manchmal ist das schon ein Scheißjob. Frankfurter Allgemeine Zeitung, 14 February 2011.

Seliger, Marco (2011b): Sterben für Kabul. Aufzeichnungen über einen verdrängten Krieg. Mittler: Hamburg.

Seliger, Marco (2010a): Das 20-Millimeter-Argument. Loyal – Magazin für Sicherheitspolitik, 7/8, pp. 30-33.

Seliger, Marco (2010c): Vom Kriege. Loyal – Magazin für Sicherheitspolitik, 10, pp. 6-17.

Shea, Neil (2012): Ready for a fight. German soldiers´ Afghan Mission shifts from Reconstruction and Training to Engaging Enemy. Stars and Stripes, 9 January 2012, pp. 16-17.

Spangenberg, André (2011): Das kleine Wunder von Nawabad. Mitteldeutsche Zeitung, 26 September 2011.

Spangenberg, André (2011): Omed heißt Hoffnung. Bundeswehr stoppt geplante Taliban-Sommeroffensive in Kundus. dpad, September 2011.

Weigelt, Julia (2013): Der einsame Kämpfer. Loyal – Magazin für Sicherheitspolitik, 3, pp. 6-11.

Weigt, Jürgen (2009): Wie hält man das aus? Beobachtungen aus dem Afghanistan-Einsatz. Österreichische Militärzeitschrift, 5, pp. 596-602.

Wüstner, André (2013): Kundus – ein Name, der sich eingebrannt hat. Die Bundeswehr – Magazin der DBwV, 11, p. 25.

List of Abbreviations

AICV	Armored Infantry Combat Vehicle
APC	Armored Personnel Carrier
BM	Ballistic Missile
CG	Counter Gerät
COIN	Counterinsurgency
DEU	Deutschland
EOD	Explosive Ordnance Disposal
IED	Improvised Explosive Device
ISAF	International Security Assistance Force
LGAN	Lehrgang General-/Admiralstabsdienst national
MEDEVAC	Medical Evacuation
Milan	Missile d'Infanterie léger antichar
NCO	non-commissioned officer
PRT	Provincial Reconstruction Team
QRF	Quick Reaction Force
RS	Resolute Support
US	United States

Additional Information

Facebook.com/DerUnsichtbareVeteran

www.Die-Neuen-Veteranen.wg.vu

Vortrag
Fotopräsentation
Diskussion

200 Tage Kunduz – Erfahrungen einer Kampfkompanie in Afghanistan

Mittwoch,
05. Dezember 2012
ab 18:30 Uhr
Hörsaal 1

der Helmut-Schmidt Universität/
Universität der Bundeswehr Hamburg,
holstenhofweg 85, 22043 Hamburg

Hauptmann Dipl.-Päd. Marcel Bohnert war von Juni 2011 bis Januar 2012 Chef einer Infanteriekompanie in der Task Force Kunduz. Während dieser Zeit war er mit seinen Frauen und Männern verantwortlich für die Sicherheit im Unruhedistrikt Chahar Darreh. In seinem Vortrag gewährt der Referent sehr persönliche Einblicke in den gefährlichen Alltag deutscher Soldatinnen und Soldaten in Kunduz.

www.200-Tage-Kunduz.wg.vu

Carola Hartmann Miles-Verlag
Politik, Gesellschaft, Militär

Marcel Bohnert, Lukas J. Reitstetter (Hrsg.), *Armee im Aufbruch. Zur Gedankenwelt junger Offiziere in den Kampftruppen der Bundeswehr,* Berlin 2014.

Jéronimo L. S. Barbin, *Imperialkriegführung im 21. Jahrhundert. Von Algier nach Bagdad. Die kolonialen Ursprünge der COIN-Doktrin,* Berlin 2015.

Dirk Freudenberg, *Counterinsurgency. Aufstandsbekämpfung als Phase zur Überwindung schwacher Staatlichkeit und zur Etablierung des Aufbaus einer stabilen Nachkriegsordnung,* Berlin 2016.

Marcel Bohnert, Björn Schreiber (Hrsg.), *Die unsichtbaren Veteranen. Kriegsheimkehrer in der deutschen Gesellschaft,* Berlin 2016.

Alois Bach, Walter Sauer (Hrsg.), *Schützen, Retten, Kämpfen – Dienen für Deutschland,* Berlin 2016.

Dirk Freudenberg, Stephan Maninger, *Neue Kriege. Sicherheitspolitische Rahmenbedingungen, Mentalitäten, Strategien, Methoden und Instrumente,* Berlin 2016.

Einsatzerfahrungen

Kay Kuhlen, *Um des lieben Friedens willen. Als Peacekeeper im Kosovo,* Eschede 2009.

Sascha Brinkmann, Joachim Hoppe (Hrsg.), *Generation Einsatz, Fallschirmjäger berichten ihre Erfahrungen aus Afghanistan,* Berlin 2010.

Artur Schwitalla, *Afghanistan, jetzt weiß ich erst… Gedanken aus meiner Zeit als Kommandeur des Provincial Reconstruction Team FEYZABAD,* Berlin 2010.

Uwe Hartmann, *War without Fighting? The Reintegration of Former Combatants in Afghanistan seen through the Lens of Strategic Thought,* Berlin 2014.

Rainer Buske, *KUNDUZ. Ein Erlebnisbericht über einen militärischen Einsatz der Bundeswehr in Afghanistan im Jahre 2008*, Berlin ²2016.

Standpunkte und Orientierungen

Daniel Giese, *Militärische Führung im Internetzeitalter – Die Bedeutung von Strategischer Kommunikation und Social Media für Entscheidungsprozesse, Organisationsstrukturen und Führerausbildung in der Bundeswehr*, Berlin 2014.

Dirk Freudenberg, *Auftragstaktik und Innere Führung. Feststellungen und Anmerkungen zur Frage nach Bedeutung und Verhältnis des inneren Gefüges und der Auftragstaktik unter den Bedingungen des Einsatzes der Deutschen Bundeswehr*, Berlin 2014.

Uwe Hartmann (Hrsg.), *Lernen von Afghanistan. Innovative Mittel und Wege für Auslandseinsätze*, Berlin 2015.

Fouzieh Melanie Alamir, *Vernetzte Sicherheit – Quo Vadis?*, Berlin 2015.

Hartwig von Schubert, *Integrative Militärethik. Ethische Urteilsbildung in der militärischen Führung*, Berlin 2015.

Uwe Hartmann, *Hybrider Krieg als neue Bedrohung von Freiheit und Frieden. Zur Relevanz der Inneren Führung in Politik, Gesellschaft und Streitkräften*, Berlin 2015.

Klaus Beckmann, *Treue.Bürgermut.Ungehorsam. Anstöße zur Führungskultur und zum beruflichen Selbstverständnis in der Bundeswehr*, Berlin 2015.

Florian Beerenkämper, Marcel Bohnert, Anja Buresch, Sandra Matuszewski, *Der innerafghanische Friedens- und Aussöhnungsprozess*, Berlin 2016.

www.miles-verlag.jimdo.com